The Magpie and the Child

The Magpie and the Child

CATRIONA CLUTTERBUCK

Wake Forest University Press

First North American edition

© Catriona Clutterbuck, 2021

For permission, write to
Wake Forest University Press
Post Office Box 7333
Winston-Salem, NC 27109
wfupress.wfu.edu
wfupress@wfu.edu

ISBN 978-1-930630-95-6 (paperback)
LCCN 2020941721

Designed and typeset
by Nathan Moehlmann,
Goosepen Studio & Press

Publication of this book was generously
supported by the Boyle Family Fund.

Printed in Canada

To my daughter
Emily Elise Wilson
(2002–2013)
and to all
who have loved her

Contents

PART TWO: THRENODIES FOR EMILY

The Magpie and the Child

You dance on her first window box that's stuffed with the green
growth of Seeds Assorted she tipped in a careless shower.
I've come from sleep on this bright summer Sunday in June
to the vicious rap of your beak on our window pane.
Fogged in dream still, I stare at the iron hook of the reaper
who's burst from his far future season of proper care
to trample all over our rough-tended flowers of belief
that no harm will come to the child who sleeps overhead
who is turning her head to the light of her own risen years.
You peck with such fury, such dark intent at the shape
of the other that only you can see in the glass:
yourself, poor bird—or is it me raised up to slaughter
the lamb of imagination whose blood I here daub
on the trembling lintel of faith that she will be spared?

(Summer 2005)

Part One: The Dry Mouth

The Dry Mouth

There was my brother and me
bringing eight heifers home
from Modeshil for the mart
the day before I left for England.

We came to cloudy black sloes
in the green branches above us.
"Can you eat those?" I asked.
"Do you remember nothing at all," he said,
"from when you were a child?"

So I bit in and got the dry mouth
that I'd forgotten for years.
I sucked at it over The Islands bridge,
the road bright in the sun, the leaves still on.

I put three berries in my pocket.
I knew this morning would come,
lying in a new bed after dawn,
sloes nuggeting in my mind
against the dry mouth.

Slievenamon

The light of May articulates it;
in July, in August, this land folds itself

away into blended haze. Now from the top hill,
saucer rim of my place, the valley lies down

and back into Leinster, Comeraghs, Galtees,
but most into nearest Slievenamon—

axle-point. It is the full of the back of the eyes
all the time we are turned away, it moves

every day in the soft seat of our tongue—
it is near, it is far, it is simply gone;

it suckles the fat land gathering stone to its nipple—
cairn of Fionn for the hard milk of fullness;

so add a stone when you reach there, tired,
the climb on a stone causeway

a pilgrimage to rival Patrick's,
a pull southwards in the dialogue towards Oisín.

Look now, the mountain has gone missing again—
you sit staring instead at a stage curtain of grey;

you know (through sufficient looking)
that if you walk through its folds

you will walk into nothing and through the air
the trees will continue to the sea.

Dorset

Its hills appease me
like the negotiated comfort feeds
of a hardy child
nurtured on thick and thin
who will spend her life seeking
such button studs in time
as this cornfield by brown lea
under a wind-sharpened sun,
and finding them, wonder,
how is here a familiar sight?

The Pond Field

The cock pheasant shot skyways from Brigid's-cross reeds
in the pond field we stalked as children, palming flies
with long grasses from the still brown lid of the water,
inletted. Each journey there, squelch and suck of
black wellington stuck and tug at it with both hands, panicking
and there was a day I stepped out into muck and went skittering
around the velvet wet, the sodden earth, in my skin
or if there wasn't such a day there could have been.
It must have been Spring mostly—jam-jars, on the hunt for spawn,
so my jumper's always too hot, the wool slightly steaming
or the field steaming in the first real heat of the year
baking crusts on the clay cliffs by the water
where cattle's feet had scored deep the dank edge.

I'm still developing these acres around the house
for the brown-headed child that slides across my brain:
myself or part of me, more like myself than me,
coming back after years in stamped prints from my skull
slipping free and floating right-side up to my side.
Insects dance on the meniscus of the past.
"Pastoral," some will say, "sun squints in a shallow pool."
"Palming flies," I'll maintain, "from the still, brown surface."

First Firelights

1.

Where the grain of the table runs,
the surface peels;
a bench fits close to the yellow wall.
I am fitting into this day like early days,
stepping big-step into the yard, then back
to my mother working near,
nursery firelight on the red wall
where her shadow bends
to my peace each minute.
This is the second hand that scales
the air of thirty years:
old ashes in the cracks of the fireplace back,
grained in. We do not, then, carry
this world on our backs—
oh the world, this day, is carrying me.

2.

I was a wet eel in the stone kitchen sink,
the white clawed bathtub too far and too big;
I was lifted the two steps to the towel
that aired on the chair by the fire
while shadows grew from the bulb in the ceiling.

An eel was in the rain barrel by the shed:
they told me "Monster, keep away, don't look in";
one day my brother held my legs so I could peep
at sluggy green, bluey brown, eyes of red
that moved like oil at my scream.

3.

Conspirators by the red ash of the kitchen,
my grandfather at seventy and me at three;

it's dead of night and we are quietly listening
through one waxy ear-plug apiece to the BBC.

Above our heads, rush of footsteps, urgent orders—
doctors and my mother's scream of pain

as my shadow slips once more down the stairs
through the cold hall and door to the big chair

to stretch bare feet to the heat by him,
our skulls touching to hear the world's service.

4.

I'd climb a chair to lie down full-length
on the high broad mantel over the fire

so I could slip my own reflection
playing hide-and-go-seek in its light.

Through the cold window, the starry yard
and the fir trees feathering the moon

watched them hunt me through the dark hour
I lay silent over crackling wood,

unfound, and getting lonelier not to win.

Exposure

The first aerial photograph
taken of us unawares
beavered us *recto* and *verso* into view —

our spring-straggly gardens,
muck of farmyards behind
and in between,

the strange valleys of our roof
above the bedroom windows'
falling blinds.

So often since then
we've slipped the house
that stopped the wind from Slievenamon

only to seek its shelter again
in the face
of the indifferent fields.

Blood Lines

With an odd name, family trees are easy-grows.
Ours spurted back through four centuries
on a force-feed of other people's work,
up time tunnels, cousins uncovered like ants,
strange American handshakes on our doorstep.
My Granddad in his eighties used to grin wickedly—
"'Lot of dirt at the bottom of those auld trees."
Now it's come to the sheet of A3 in the drawer
and its blood drip from fifteen-something to my Dad.

I held that paper in my hand tonight, saw it
turn to thin-stretched skin, saw through it
waving all the silhouettes of the obliterated,
blanched branches of a thousand families
grey heaped behind the names of wives, calling;
and thickening in my hand
all the sharded-off daughters and sisters,
their erased children swinging beneath them,
young husbands, dead babies on inked fork heads,
stone growing back in the chiseled grooves
of their names.

The page in my hand became itself again,
a pinball machine's intricate descent,
and I saw where into it will fit
my name, my sister's name—the vertical drop
into our descendants whitened out.
Our great-granddaughters. Waiting.
One day I will follow the vein
to my mother's mother's mother and beyond.
Paint in the ghosts that walk in my heels.

In the Emergency

This is the story my mother has told
of when her father died during the Emergency:
the gentle horse-lover lifted too heavy a load
for his heart attacked next day and sundered.

She and her sister were in school that morning,
and when the messenger came to call them,
one was learning to sing of old Ireland free;
the other being slapped for getting her sums wrong.

Two girls walking back the dappled way home
meet a neighbor and ask her in worry—
"Ah there's no more about him, the poor man, he's gone," they are told
and learn their time through its highroad of sorrow.

His last words—"Do you think that they ever come back?"
And his own answer: "I think they do... but they don't talk."
Soon his jaw was bound tight, him still where he'd sat,
when my mother entered and made to fly to him

but was yanked by her pigtails, held from behind
for fear of her fear and her love for him—
yet though waked all that night, left not one moment alone,
still his animals sickened and died for him...

Sixty years on, his child tells out this thing
in her kitchen once evening jobs are done
to a daughter who'd never heard the story before
yet has sensed it by heart since her own life began.

Writing My Initials

I am four. Started school.
My big brother is drawing
with his black nib
two standing curves—CC.
"These mean you," he tells me
but I'm crying,
"No! No! No!"

*

I can draw apples—
with the Master's hand around my hand
we are singing: "She'll be coming
round the mountain when she comes"—
my pencil's sweeping and widening
as I spiral, curve on curve…

*

I have forked my own tongue.
In its folds the mirror words slip;
the coding is fear
where these silent ones swim.
Seat-of-need's a tangle,
Tom's-a-cold.
My red soul's shrunk in
where the sly slide of the grill
across my dark-boxed truth
runs smooth, runs grooved
for half-lunged, fish-tailed, I—

When I opened the red door in the garden wall,
I faced the bull coming towards me
in my child's cotton dress, my brothers
pursuing behind. And I turned and ran.

All that day I spent alone in the hay-barn
spelling out to myself "pneumonia,"
drawing its silent "p" across my tongue
like a bull through the eye of a needle.

*

The shadow of me
undressing
is cast against the wall.
Each night I'm bigger than I am,
curved, my hair sticks out.
No matter how I turn
I will always be
flat, dark against the light
and I move most gracefully
on the wall.

Rib

When God took a rib out of man
and made it up into woman,
he left the cage of man's heart unfinished,
missing one bar, undone.

Though he closed the place over with flesh,
inside there is still a gap,
a breach in his perfect enclosure,
a loneliness after her flight.

Eve was made of one rib,
one long curved half-circle of bone;
inside in her upright flesh,
not sin but original shape,

of cup, boat, letter, hut, mouth,
moon sliver—deliberate half-closures;
she collected up space in her curve,
threw earth from her wide open side.

Martha Blake Reprieved

(after Austin Clarke)

Morning light on the chancel crucifix
throws the shadow of the body of Christ
to the wall before her in duplicate,
like those thieves cast to either side

who have claimed for her more and less
than her chance of eternal life
in love that makes its home in her flesh
through His broken legs opening wide

to receive one whose dreams may accept
the carnal vessel emptied entire,
yet whose body would make her forget
all need for such sacrifice,

purer thought knowing body is blessed
by its hunger when satisfied—
full cupboards with loosened clasps
along her passage out of the void

of substance in poetry's pity
that has held her last breath disappointed:
may her life instead be remitted
by grace of the least of its creaturely joys.

Queens of the May

Mayday. White afternoon light
in the white mouth of the year.

Follow a blue thread of sound
to the braid of girls
in their convent-school years
song-circling the stations of faith—

grey chapel and tennis court,
silver graveyard and Canon's Walk,

towering beech trees
baby-greening ajar
the cervix of summer
above our mantilla'd heads.

Hear it again, our petition
in the hymn of our changing flesh:
bring flowers of the rarest
and blossoms the fairest…

The Break-Up

His presence, his half-presence, a fantail of sparks
in the darkroom of her body: bellows wheel
in a broad hearth carried hand beyond hand
as he surged through her first catch of flame.
And this is the wave of it, flowing back:
the very tips of his fingers' sure trickle
while over and over he takes the time…
A machine comes round in circles of some field
beyond this suburb, its roar growing and ebbing,
and she is strange, like roses.

*

He's like a piece of wood she can't leave down
but she doesn't know where to put him:
each joist of her life where she tries him for size
seems to resist him. How we are grained!
She remembers the wise woman's words—
"He may lie with your body, my girl,
but woman, does he lie with your mind?"

*

What she remembers the night he left
is the air-brush of autumn on her skin
and the punts tied vacant on the water.
September pulled the weft out of the basket of this love.
He tied his clock to the apple tree, out of time.
It's the moon, not the miles, has swung him
this far astray of her, stalemate
creeping over them like figs.

Carved Head at Jerpoint

At first look, it's a mason's whim:
two long and delicate lines
chiseled to perfect balance
each side of his apple-round cheeks.

But this man's entwined in no Eden:
look again—limbs are twisted and tied
to a crossbeam strapped to his shoulders
so his neck muscles scream for release,

drowning out the sweet pulse of forgetting
of self in the stretched arms of praise
of St. Kevin nestling the blackbird
in a hand extended in cruciform.

No chicks can fly from the other's clenched palms
held in agony by human decree:
his yoke scores the flesh of each century still
seeking substance in enmity—

Kilcooley

Abbey—open, empty,
nests in your sides,
your great East Window
exfoliating sky.

*

The mermaid of Kilcooley
waits inside the transcept door,
her burnished tail a flicker
of a world to be restored.

*

The Weeper Apostles
guard a Butler tomb
still grieving for the loss
of Kilcooley's looser rule.

*

Against high odds of their undoing
had one chisel tap slipped,
craftsmen raised these figures
as all surrounding stone was stripped.

*

Another church in cruciform—
four rose windows, one each end;
in Gortnahoe we gather
falling petals in amends.

*

In the bleak midwinter
during mass for Christmas Eve
earth grew soft with shimmer
of snowfall over Glengoole.

*

The chapel at Bawnlea
where the Palatines once prayed
is since a milking parlor—
nurture in exchange.

*

Before dawn on Easter Sunday
a pilgrim chain of lights
creeps through bog to Derrynaflan,
retrieving hope in Christ.

*

Each midday Sunday churchyard
offering weathered stones
as den to scattering children
outraces gravity in the bone.

Passing On the Faith

(*i.m. Angela Clutterbuck, 1932–2017*)

"He spat on the ground, made a paste with the spittle, put this over
the eyes of the blind man, and said to him, 'Go and wash.'" (John 9: 6–7)

The church in Ballingarry
still bears the black pressure
of belief at breaking point
as it conforms

to roof beams crossed and jointed
into screws' black bite,
driving the ante of our credence
into brace.

Into its door-thudded silence
my mother and I
must come once more
to queue in prismed air;

here I'll ask her forgiveness,
though long ago freely given,
to release the clutch of my mistrust
in Faith that cleaved

to the ancient name of the Third Person
of the Holy Trinity
broken off her children's tongues
in primary school,

leaving her fathers' faith unspoken
and our mother kneel alone
with us as wraiths re-dressed
in comfort-rags of hope—

"You'd never know what King might reign then,"
she would say,
trusting us even to the image
of God abandoned,

that we reform in His spit
as the slime off our own day,
giving up the Ghost for us
at that miry crossroads

where rut-locked religion softens
under her love's untold, lightest touch,
to the mud in all our eyes
through which we'll see again.

Cinders

The block through the guard is still glowing
when I come down from lying awake in the dark
to wait out the small hours alone.
I watch its glimmer-pulse through thickening grey skin
as it lets itself go, becoming its own seed and end,
clucking itself to pieces. A tiny whistle
as its red eye opens for a moment
to take me in—then recovers itself in dust.

Evictions

1.
Barr an Domhain. The top of the world.
Cabins built stone over stone.
Half-doors, lintels, hearths
banked and smoldering through each dark.

Castlemorris. Wrought iron gates
and avenue arrowing to the big house.
The townland tiptoeing past,
gates closing behind the box carriage.

Battering-ram then and row of constables;
dust of generations as the thatch collapsed
in house after house, tenants clenched and staring,
then a priest's voice high over the crack of timber:

There'll be fires in Barnadown
when the fires in Castlemorris are all dead!
—Children creep now in the great gates
for blackberries thick by the drive

that points to a field where grass flows
over the humped lines of formal gardens,
fire-cracked stones cold and spread for outhouses
where each evening smoke clears in the top country.

(1994)

2.

Yet how can I know what happened there,
stumbling in the very name's dark gap?
I raised Barnadown to Barr an Domhain
and telescoped its smoldering hearths

through the rust-locked great gates of story,
origins beckoning in worn props of shame —
with a battering ram and a row of constables,
I re-built the fire-cracked stones of lost pain

of a people in dust, a generation done
to death as those thatches collapsed,
and thrilled to them clenched for victory
through ameliorative voice over timber's crack:

There'll be fires in Barnadown
when the fires in Castlemorris are all dead!
—so cast to adumbrate, they are ebonized,
those tenants for whom that occasion of curse

re-ignites in these rites of mis-witness
from the right side of time, that allow
their townlands of truth be razed again
to a minstrel show in Mnemosyne's big house.

(2004)

Autumn Equinox

Light stretched, thinned, clear
as the days contract

over the field-line
towards winter.

Light offered
and the salver withdrawn:

light as a harvest
both won and lost

of which we take stock
whilst still

in the day's
unassailable light.

Solstices

A field-thrum hay orbit
hatching the Ten Acres,
a tractor radiator,
dog pant on a dark patch:

summer turned
on this spit,
bird flick against light
louvring open the sky

and deepest green,
eight at evening
where the long grass
stands uncombed
and clothes stir
over the currant bushes,
dried, forgotten.

Inside, anthracite stirs;
heat curls the sticky strips
where flies struggle
and the clock ticks

towards winter—
the chainsaw bawling
like a bullock from the shed
as crows call
through the hard air.

Spring Equinox

About now the light seems to reverse,
sun dodging for days behind clouds
in *fort/da* game with its promise of heat,
crying wolf to my long winter's hope.
Three deer have come down from the trees
only to turn back across the line
of their over-extended confidence
where our snowman, browbeaten by rain,
sank his head at last into grass.

Insects tremble in cobwebs of wind.
I've mistaken the first sight of midges
for the snowflakes of lingering winter
even as the bale-elevator of summers past
clacks back to mechanical life,
its spiked chain in diagonal loop
rising to me still learning to stand
and receive, then swing to the dark
of the rick slowly filling my span,
the packed growth I'd overlooked
of each irregular season I've borne.

Count my years as non-transitive dice
stored for me in the barns of God
so that, head hung at the Judgement seat
when my final inventory is cast,
I am spared by their *non-sequitur*:
no sum is final in love's renewed throw.
Let even this promise then clack behind me
like the stick a running child pulls
against the iron railings of winter,
receding… till at last overcome.

My Father Making Shapes
for his Grown Children, Visiting

(*i.m. James Clutterbuck, 1933–2019*)

Cue his stage-entrance crash through the warped back door,
the wall behind him dinted with care,
into the kitchen where we laze over late tea and toast—
"Make a shape! There's the world to do out there!"

His work litany reloads that's taught us all to run
daily exercising anxiety
'round the dog-track that we carve about the edges of the undone,
fulfilled only ever provisionally.

Driving from the city, we ease the clutch of our commitment
into the groove of his hope we'll go beyond him—
a seven-months child who crossed too early his own line of fate,
hating his full-term never-self's shiny achieving.

On home ground, we still hold these shadows to our throats
in light side-glancing across time's messy table
towards a child's hand drawing fate in a thread from his work-coat,
the shape of our lives from his tangled cat's cradle

whose slipknot solves as sudden as this morning's cool and grey
where the cement paths we daily tread once more spill over
into the spring-cusped mucky farmyard on a translucent day
where he's making for the warped back door—

Elegy at Pentecost

(i.m. Liam O'Cinnéide, 1962–1983)

1.

I couldn't stay in the deep sleep I pulled around me
last night. When I willed myself back to the sleep-pen
I found you behind the gate: the square's mizzle again,

your brothers lifting you shoulder high and horizontal
for the two hundred yards to the cathedral door,
its high spire holding out in mid-air above you.

Why now, after years? Not wistful, not worried, not sad:
last night you were nowhere in my mind.
You were nowhere.

2.

Flat bottomed blue boat frets and spars
a yard from the crank of your kneeling body
drawing a slimed iron chain through your hands,

timed with the snaffle in the canal reeds' static,
the repeating swish of denim between your thighs.
You draw a wake of green water through the years

where the elaborate insects make their home,
the original, single-celled species of love—
And it's evening, sliding through, singing

row row row your boat far beyond the Black Bridge,
river wide as continents and as dark and as deep…
Cycle me across the sleeping city, crash the silent lights,

tauten your knuckles to take the curve of the college,
the flaps of your dufflecoat coming to rest,
my shadow on your crossbar dimming to white.

3.

In the early days of June, talking fire:
your "lights that light the darkness
and do not scorch the darkness" —

Was it so? Light over your fair head
drawing you out beyond your fear
to the place where you knew

no one would come, no one take
you back, your final bright talk
with a tongue of flame?

4.

your death the quarry
where I go again to draw
the shape of nothing

to sift a fine comb
through the mulberry bushes
of over and done

to walk further rounds
of this ground for the tart smell
that stone earth throws off

5.

Graced gold, old skin, first love —
dust from your temple of absence
once filled my rubbery lungs.

Now may I follow you who's flown
beyond the forming griefs that killed you,
offering at last something more than remembrance:

dance with me, old shadow—
everything we were, we become once again:
scald-crow, blackbird in flight, testing old wings.

Engagement Walk, Summer 1999

Together into the noontime-empty street and uphill
to where four roads meet, turning left between fields of rape
to the sign pointing straight through stubble. Over the hill then
to the swish and the crackle of heads uncut against
my green skirt and the sun on his shoulder snared
in his grey-brown speckled hair, on his backs' elastic
moving across a land throwing open its rooms to us:
days of bounty spring in our feet, taking first step
across the seal of the century's end. Oxfordshire yields
its high horizon—from the Ridgeway, greying wheat,
head-bent and rattling, kneels to a combine's spread lips
roaring grain to the trailer beneath, confident
beyond waste or the death of hope. On then to Blewbury's
tunnel of sloes in god-motherly heat, so much fruit within reach.

October

Leaves whirl on tarmac
like children around the yard.
The years run like leaves.

Miscarriage

By then you were a bean shape curled into yourself,
the books said, and were wrong. You'd made yourself
an empty sac attached to the wall of my womb,
but declined to enter it. For the three weeks
after the clear blue line when he and I read and schemed
and distributed our secret in careful increments,
you were hesitating, then turning to leave.
Bags of salt water cushion the shape you've left,
doubled-back crease, cloud of cell-space,
this new and certain knowledge that my body
and his can start this, that mine or yours can finish it
in a cold jelly probe moved by the nurse inside me,
my blood and yours staining the sheet-role brown.
My held breath that morning was for the tight-rope walk
past the waiting room's bumps to phone him,
and weeks later, this flittering with balloons
called week eleven, week twelve, homes I'd built
for you in the air, in the marked diary I've thrown away
now all the grief I've known is welcoming you in.

The Obstetrician's Waiting Room

We sit silent here on hard-backed upright chairs;
Alice takes our cards from a box when we come in.
We place our bodies into cradles of his care.

We change places month to month in shifting layers;
move to our next-in-line stick-out-stomach kin
to sit silent once again on hard-backed chairs

holding new out-of-date *Hellos* so we can stare
at sleek mounds of paper women who won't thicken
like our bodies cradled in his bony care

while we eye from underneath what each one wears
to vex the conclave of our silence by fastening
one to the other packed together here on chairs

in closed contract with the moment that we dared
let love or fear or need or pain, yang or yin
carve our bodies to these boned cradles of care

waiting out the long weeks until they tear
and open wide for the unforeseeable child we believe we win
by sitting silent here on hard-backed upright chairs,
bone-bearing bodies into cradles through his care.

Thirty-Five Weeks

Dark is closing the thirty-five weeks
since my last legitimate confession of blood.

Age-of-Christ belly hangs low, hand-held
in my slow walk from room to room.

Evening bird call of late-April wind and rain
skins the last of the cow of this long winter pregnancy.

I crouch in the house of my coming child,
the webs of this cocoon life in my mouth.

The dead weight in my middle turns to snake-
wave of head and backbone under my hand.

The muscles of my will slacken
and dream themselves ready for opening.

I will burn the nightdress of this quarter life
I live in, masquerading for the whole.

Squinching, thumping, drumming one,
make more vacuums with your fists and heels

in the silt lake where I'm waiting for you.

Salmon

The sea is free and cold
where you lived beyond conception.

Gills flickered my taste and you turned
to nuzzle my dusty interior.

You slipped the torn driftnets hung
for your sibling flushed out on the tide;

swam past the laborious flies
I cast each month from the shallows of fear.

You are in me now leaping weirs
towards the pool of your spirit-sinew

that churns with the silts of your spawning
freshly breaking through.

Late Pregnancy

We flex
towards the unknown name
of our air-bubble baby
who slips sideways
through the hole
in your guitar,
the keeper-ring
tightening on my finger,
the nozzle
of the scanning machine.
Magpies step unevenly
through my stomach
while the wind tugs
distractedly at our roof.
The child blindly feels
the braille knobs
of my womb
as I sit in séance
and wait—
a depth-charge kick
into the clockwork
of my days,
a groundswell raising
my hand in praise.

The Stolen Boat

When it was time, she snuggled beyond call,
pulling my tired muscles further round
as she dropped to the bottom of my hold.
Who could blame her? My trick cyclist
up-ended, her pedals now trapped in fold.
I watched the buoy of her due date sail past
who could have sworn us at anchor-hold
on the long arm of the Y of my pelvis,
a wishbone bending under her load.

I woke at dawn to the frisk of the engine,
a slow propeller gathering whisks of pain;
a cool grey morning, sea-calm, tide running
for a woman holding the tiller of her stomach.
I began to get the feel of the bigger waves
and started to tack and to turn for home
between the bolsters of reddening spume.

But I ran aground on the reef of their fear
that soon snared 'round my báidín-ó
laid down and bared for the scalpel's teeth
that entered me—a pirate's cut without words.
My hide screamed as her fair head was nicked
to check the colors of the waters of the moon
while I was wired to the stare of the sun
and her heart pounded all day in the room.

That evening, the opening drawstrings stuck
that had been jerked from behind the drug screen
splitting me from myself, so they cut
a permanent smile just above the water's reach
into which pale hands moved with skill

to uncurl her from me stretched beneath
who cast in vain for her with eyehooks.
How I latched to her, ached for her heft!
Masked fishermen caulked the wound.

Hunger

In the deep night you stir for food,
twist the bands of your loosening sleep.

I awake and reach for you and you curl,
a stiff S of updrawn knees,

arched back and back-thrown head
as you rise through the dark to me.

I fuss with pillows to your urgent breath,
your silk head smacking from side to side,

hunger smothering you out there in the dark
till I draw you horizontal to my breast,

your opening fish mouth gasping onto me,
your sharp mews suddenly silenced.

You suck with no break
the deep massage pulls on the grape;

I hear the milk squirt in the chasm
of your hungry mouth while your near leg rises

and kicks the air, cloth feet cycling the hill
of your father's dark oblivious shoulder.

The dim light shines on the spider who pauses
then begins again its journey across the floor.

You click your jaws to your five-second pattern,
catch your life's breath three times in relief.

The Prism

Switch her morning-dark body round:
sweet like the hard-sucked honeysuckle,
she lets my nipple escape like a mouse
to turn swiftly on it and stare at me, busy.

She glares at me in her late hour of whimpers
till my mother takes her, and for her sake
once more gives voice: "Here I am again,
passed around like snuff at a wake."

I stand between them, longing to be
the skipped generation of three
—a red admiral fluttering free
of this sticky web growing all around me—

but she blows me bubbles to buzz me back in
to the deep room I will live within.
My life, my white light, within this prism:
your head is tucked beneath my chin.

Woman Commuting

You sit on the toilet seat at just three years old,
your Dad kneeling to the tears that stream from your face.

You're crying for me who am telling you I have to go,
bending to kiss you once more whilst washing my hands.

The swelling inside to have woken you up hours before,
to hold you and murmur you into the light of this day

is seen off by the early bird's rancorous screaming for worms
in the mind of a woman who works at crossing out lists.

You want only me but I have already gone:
near the city now, your wail has stilled in my ears;

the child opposite me is giggling at game with her mam
and I know you'll be fine, by now crossing over my fears

of the shadow attaching itself to you, learning helplessness
in your mute understanding that I must have wanted to leave —

The Return

I drive through the center of Oxford today
with my child fast asleep in the back,

along St. Giles, up the Banbury Road, past myself
fiercely cycling the other track

who must be late for a bite or a book and intent
on an hour that's ten years in the past,

yet that's held in this honey hole intact
as her wheels that are twisted by cobbles

swerve too close to the older me who stares
through her shadow that's crossing my screen

so I call out loud to my oblivious child
to look, look! oh heart's love, right here

is where your other mother is about to slide
on the black ice of the turn of her thirties

to land without knowing her imprint will take
in this riddled ground that has held her

long levering in love with another life
she would yearn across oceans and years,

while your real mother left, came to her senses to turn
towards the breath that's in your breath, my dear,

who sleeps as I pass by the time of my life
with these ghosts who've gone into your making,

unreal for me now in this day but most real
for me still in that season I see now

whirl and suck 'round you to lose itself
like the truth in my rear-view mirror.

Daughter at Dawn

Thump on the boards and pat-pat-pat
of her feet in the early morning dark
to our bed and its warmth, kneading my side
as though, here, she were trying to get back

to where the light on the curve of her closed eyelids,
her widow's peak above the pillow's folds,
parted lips breathing in all her day will hold
were but a dream of being lost to this world.

Trompe L'Oeil

Once from work, I came to in the college computer room
to keys that tapped all around me like the rain;
I looked up to the skylight to enjoy that fancy's loot
only to find myself alone under the spotted pane.

Years later I saw my small child running outside in the dark—
my lungs clamped shut, suddenly locking me out
till I realized she'd been passing right behind my back,
her ghost in the glass the escapee that mocked my fright.

At the Site of Bowen's Court

Overshot—but this time we turn
back into the bowl of Farrahy
filling in the late August afternoon.

The avenue swings from our sight
through a field barred "No Entry,"
so we find the churchyard alongside.

Our small daughter climbs over graves
to touch the sheen of the laurel leaves
above the plot of a young servant girl

while I move restlessly failing to find
the tall stone shadowed against the back wall
with the dash in her bracketed name.

He points to it and leaves me to attend
a world not yet over—as I know now I'll be
when the light too will fall through my name

some summer that burns to throw
one such last perfect day for the child
who'll by then have pulsed from my hand

like the laurel-leaf kite
she's now scribbling on air
alongside me and won't let go—

(August 2006)

Menopause

Sycamore on black through the glass
of the half-landing
frantic to flee this stormy night...

On track for the body's winter,
its savage feeding ground,
I weave a blanket for sleep:

my unborn children kneading
their heels in my side
and my bloodline ribboning the road

in every leaf at last
broken for earth
under tomorrow's clear grey sky.

Part Two: Threnodies for Emily

White light exploding thin line over the world
and high as can go, a pure milky white
filling everything—
and still the traffic comes, morning sits on every surface,
a crow calls, cutlery rattles in the kitchen
and a keyboard begins to patter-jab.

*

crossing and cutting
this glass pane
folding in on itself

the moments
cut by birdsong or flight
every day since

you were waked
and for the first time
the sharp clear chirp

of some small bird
came calling
clear and sharp

*

I stare hard at the space you stood by
to take your leave just a while ago,
wanting only to push back through time
and touch you to turn from your course,

to hold you once more in my arms,
reluctant-pleased as I know you'd be—
but see a swift cut across the span
of this world I will you would seek:

a bird that won't land on the earth
for fear of wounding its wings
and so feeds and sleeps without perch
in the free air to which it clings,

who just flicks at the pain of this cup
handed to me to overflowing,
turns forked tail, like your two thumbs up
discharging me, "Stay with my going!"

*

The mirror on the landing is full to the brim
with her passing, milky light digesting
its shiver.

The shadows of the big hall window frame
are squaring off the light
behind the blind.

*

We three once swayed in harness in the company of traffic,
side vision laying down a reel of broken medium strip;
our driver restless in his seat against the tedium of concentration,
his big instrument panel rattling like stocked duty-free at sea.

Cat's eyes blinked in daylight as together we held the camber,
being carried in suspension, all our hopes stowed beneath,
ignoring tremor in our feet and rattle through our frames
as we went *tock–tock* over all those sectioned concrete bits.

The road we two once traveled was the sound of one heartbeat
in a chest reached for and tested to guard against fever's heat,
not knowing we'd be left abandoned at its unapproved stop
stumbling in shock that it should all come down to this.

*

Car swishing down the road
in early morning stillness:
a knife loosening a seam,
a bird opening a wake
through closed-over waters
—this lake I carry,
this covered and sealed-in arc—

*

I've barely begun to touch this,
yet have done so intimately:

I have lain down beside her
and cradled her heavy head,
cupping the curve of her cold shoulder
in the palm of my hand.

When her arm began to stiffen
in its place across her front,
I've helped strip and re-dress her
in newly-bought things.

I've turned her fair head towards me
so the fluids in her lungs
might spill less copiously,
then let them soak me through.

*

Dandelion fluff seeding past me in the air,
all such flying things:
two white butterflies above the rockery today
as spotted from the kitchen sink,
the swoop of a bird through the yard outside,
starlings gathering on the telephone wires,
all the summer's fine weather—

*

Water beetles twirl over the meniscus
and tiny fish turn up their silver flank to feed;
near and wide circles are kissed from beneath
while the larger surface flows with light;
a whole liquid sheet is tucked into the fringes
of these dark wooded islands and shores.

*

The meter-man
blesses himself
coming in our gate.

*

This afternoon, I lay in the garden
plucking grass stems from the sheaths of themselves
to nibble at their lower-tip sweetness
while studying the blue sky and wide clouds
and intensely thick green of the ashes and sycamores
and the hills' upward familiar sweep.

This evening, dark clouds cover the sunset
still glowing just above the horizon,
a fierce gauze alighting on the fence posts
and yellow-headed grasses of the field
slowly folding itself from our sight.

*

Rollers. Unstable cliffs.
The moon's fat glimmer on the ocean.

This chill, sweet night,
we are still within the pull
of a snarl-fight over old ground
between distance and intimacy.

All is changed, and we cannot take it in—
the expanse of sky,
the length of unbroken horizon,
the waves curling viciously towards the shore.

*

The reverberating echo
of the life that is over
in the hollow space
it has left behind

cut by two short yaps
from a dog in the distance
as a breeze gathers
and rustles around.

*

First day back at school and already I have missed
remembering the approach of home time:
the breath of air in the squeeze between worlds,
the hurried drive, the quick walk to the gates,
eyes sifting the maelstrom of blue to find her
stepping towards me, coat and hat on askew,
ready to move off beside me down the path: adjusting.
How did this duty-of-care so quickly concede?
I register the empty space all around me,
looking back at the un-retraceable world.

*

Our parenthood
is an exposed saucer of roots
at the end of a fallen tree
in the woods of home,
all its clayed-up twists and turns
shriveling into a landscape
of torn and dangling forms.

*

How strange to leave a message about you
on the Genetics Testing Unit's answering machine:
I give your details and ask them to contact us—
these unknown decoders of your late destiny.
Acridity taints my wild pleasure
at using your name in the present tense,
as though making you an overdue dental appointment
and not a request for the reason you're dead.
I would have those results delayed indefinitely
as that tiny sliver of your DNA
slips the guardianship of my sad memory
into the wider world's provenance and care,
for my heart glories in your being again relevant,
shyly affirming its greatest claim—you lived.

*

Panic-aching upsurge of desire
to be able to collect my daughter from school,
swallowed back down again
with resentment at all my former ills.

I do not know why I am here:
I'm like a child being asked to eat her greens
to absorb habits of good living
for her future's sake. But such value on its own
will not be enough—there must be
something nice after my dinner.

Listen—there is quiet outside.
A bird chirps. The system hums. The season turns.
The collapsed sun umbrella is flapping its wings.
The kitchen's heat releases itself
in odd ticks and lettings go.

*

When I used wake her on snowy days,
her first question, piling on quick layers,
was always, *Will there be school?*
We'd argue gloves while she scrunched to the car
to scrape a white pod to hurl at me,
then she'd head away up the field,
turning to check her footprints behind.

Now, first snowfall since she died,
the wind tearing flakes horizontal
as dusk comes down early
and a single blackbird pecks the ground.
Soon a blur of white outside,
the thicker flakes nearer the glass
pausing to look in as they pass.

*

My coin of good hope traveling brightly around
the rim of comfort's collection funnel
once more depreciates to the point that it veers
into the black hole towards which it's been accelerating:

I've been going about as though she were still here,
circumscribing the dark center of our home—
the grave, given truth of her empty bed
hollowing my life to an echoing drum.

*

In this, the longest night of the year in which she died,
the wind howls after dawn with rain-repeated cries
for one who gave us light through her decade in this world
till her expanding heart spun her life beyond our hold
towards a sun grown big with child, just then returned to earth
for a summer's graced weather that at last's allowed rebirth
of this country's faith in crops, well-being in kith and kin—
primal warmth we'd not deny, though permafrost close in
on *our* root and branch of vision, on scope and will and mind
to make something of living, now she is underground.

Yet as we open her friend's card to us—cut-out kings
            on a penciled road
winding towards a tiny manger with a message in its fold,
"I am sorry for how hard this Christmas time will be"—
a shaft steals down the passage past these blocks of misery
to touch the cushioned dark of a chamber scoured and zipped
against what life's a-stir outside in shivering stem and tip.
This winter's lonely child of hope in cocksteps of light
is tentative as blue in the morning's washed-out sky
that's already clouding over what it has just inferred—
first steps of our unlikely quest for life here without her.

*

"How does it feel?"

Like being ducked
as a witch

who both sinks
and swims

into the quick—

hand over hand
canceling,

forcing breath.

*

Last year I took her with me
out into the boggy field
to cut reeds to stretch the evenings
on crosses we fumbled to weave.

This year the cloth she's woven
is left out on our windowsill,
absorbing us until morning
retrieves it, drenched with Spring.

The garland of green water-bottle tops
she wore last St. Patrick's eve
hangs from the lamp in our kitchen
by the chair she used curl in and read.
Though her circuits of refreshment
are more mysterious now to me,
I will keep the rounds of her life here:
my chaplet child, my *eau de vie*.

*

Bathroom:

A bottle of Nurofen for Children, Six-Plus, orange flavored;
a white hooded baby towel, still in use;
a box with stickered label saying "Children's Meds";
a fawn-colored hairband, among others unused;
a toy black helicopter on its side gathering dust;
a tube of Sensodyne Pronamel for children;
scattered toothbrushes, assorted;
a hair grip, opened;
a green pottery water-whistling model bird;
a wooden boat with single mast and yellow sail;
an empty baking-powder tin, purpose unknown;
a soft plastic fish;
a small white funnel;
a bottle of Johnson's extra-rich baby wash;
an almost empty bottle of Jasmine Shampoo for all hair types;
a bath pillow.

I am holding my breath during these days
as if only now she was due to go,
hearing the bird again that through last May
chirped sharp as a chisel on stone.

The last of the firsts stream by me
stuck on this strange plateau,
shrink-wrapped in false equanimity,
the edge of the deep not where I was told.

Retracing last days, I call aloud
to the house martins under my eaves
to leak back to the mirror of the old world
her name, that she come home to me.

But my perpetual calendar opens
on a quest she has always held dear—
this month's lighthouse and sea a token
of my Dawntreader's voyaging dreams.

*

I shiver at the thought of one year ago
through this summer's new dress of relief—
my shield of shock then still to transpose
to the scabrous habit of all-in-one grief.

But under this year's looser linen
that sad suit's become flesh of my flesh,
chaffing now at its likelihood of living
without the child who once fed at my breast.

*

The sun is glowing inside its own shroud.
We live in one corner of a field
that once hummed with summer
whose skin is peeling back in one piece.

Meanwhile the sea rocks us, holds us, carries us,
casts us forwards on big waves rolling in.
Later we find a giant jellyfish on the shore
inside which lives one small crab, feeding.

*

We are gestating
your new life:
two pillars of stone
who once
wrapped you round
in flesh.

*

Poll na Brón—its capstone's massive slant
a runway, swallow hole, absence funnel;
its suspended impossible weight
floating free in time, while
tilted at a jaunty angle
over fields of
flowering
stone.

Rock bottom,
yet far further chasms
to go.

On Stonehaven Beach
we stood on the bank
of a small, deep river
that cut off the strand,

beside itself to pulse
to anonymity
not ten yards from us
in the cold North Sea.

My mother recalls out of the blue
my near-drowning as a teenager—
how, watching me cast on the ground
under mouth-to-mouth from a stranger,
she saw my eyes first begin to flicker.

Listening to her now, I seem to feel
sea water coming up my throat:
what was it that was given for us that day
when some force paused over me,
then nodding "Later," moved away?

*

A burning evening sun
shines low and straight
into my rear-view mirror
as a fox cuts across my path
and a lone doe
seeks a gap in the road
to escape me.

*

Our friend has dreamt
she was in an autumn wood
with yellow and gold leaves flying,
when she saw our young daughter,
long hair full of light
all swept across her forehead.

In a green sweatshirt and leggings,
the girl was up on a bank
(our friend on the path below),
and she was the leader
of a great gang
of other children whooping and following.

She stopped to ask our good friend,
Can I come to your house?—
Yes of course, I'll just call your parents.
But our child shouted *No!*
We have to go now!
There's no time for their permission!
Our friend saw before her

a huge truck on the road,
and became afraid for the young girl running:
Come down, please, now!
It's much too dangerous!
but she'd raced ahead, far too busy to worry.

(*i.m. Gobnait Uí Mhurchú*)

*

Unhome again—more and more
the strangeness of you not here

is your absence becoming familiar—
not you, but your unlived life

the shadow in our doorway
gaping at our comings and goings.

*

When Ceres lost her daughter
and grieved so much no corn would grow,
she was given an infusion of poppies

so she could forget what had happened
for long enough to regain her energy
and begin to nurture the new season.

This pen is my opium, but what knowledge
can it carry back from this frozen time,
and how much of me must it leave behind?

Oh my daughter—what I see
is only the faintest outline of your shadow
thrown by light from wherever you are.

Strange poppies have been found
by the Crag path this year,
but we've forgotten to collect their seeds.

*

"How is it now?"
No longer harrowing—
more deep-till ploughing,
going backwards,
breaking again and again to bits.

*

Ours is the parish lintel
un-daubed with the blood of the lamb:
would I not tremble at my good fortune
had I not been the one

whose child just died with no warning
in spite of all their good service could do—
defibrillators, unbroken compressions
keeping her blood on the move;

in spite of sirens and speed and bright daylight,
gates opened and space made and given;
despite the damp in the ground where she lay
that should have told her get up but she didn't;

in spite of them keeping all traffic at bay
and their children in dressing rooms;
despite calls and texts sent far and wide,
their desperate prayers said against our ruin;

despite the pace at which our friend drove us
on the heels of two ambulances
in the first of which lay our child, dying,
though technically still with a chance;

despite the best teams of medics,
their great care of her father and me;
despite a world of people's single wish
that she be brought back home to us

whole and fully recovered,
and asking for something to eat...

*

Tethered and empty
and gibbeting in space

that they grip the harder
for sight of us swinging

fitful and frozen
to the wind.

*

When I try to borrow back
even one moment of the many
in which the warm vessels
of my inner elbows

cupped themselves around
the delicate wings

of my growing child's shoulders
to draw her to me again,

it is not allowed.

*

It is as though we have been distracted
to the point that only now
have we looked behind to find her gone.

Others have done her more honor,
recalling her regularly to each other
in particular places and times.

Would I *not* have her be the one
they remember playing with their children
on a beach long ago?

Recollecting her as we cannot,
they keep us here with them
rippling towards extinction

as though we were still one of those
who, in passing,
one day will lose their children.

In my dream it is the day of the summer holidays
and it is hot. I am hanging around the school door
with a bowl full of longing I need to spill,
but another mother has slipped in before me
bearing a marvelous rosewood vessel
piled full of its own extravagantly-scented resins
of pinks and browns and fawns all marbled together.
I wake with my empty hands reaching out
for one small chunk to pick up and suck
as though never before and never again to taste
such sweetness and fullness direct from the source
I too would attend, though still holding my own.

*

Low sunlight through the church windows
casts a white disc on the altar cloth
at the end of the line of altar servers
from the team of which she was part;
they kneel on the sanctuary step
after the consecration
while we watch from the right transept
her advent light as new creation.

*

How do I, who can meet you no more in this world,
greet the world into which you are come?
You have been the earth which makes my heaven—
how now may I turn towards the real thing for good?

*

I think of walking away from this road
beyond sight or interference
through my childhood's freshly-cut
long interlinking inner hayfields,
silent and empty in their skirt of trees
under the early sun,
a single bird calling from the ditches
as my feet trip on the heavy swaths
and a breeze stirs the top strands
of the richly withering grass
lain scattered as it fell from the turner
the previous evening,
a whole winter's feed in the making,
the land quiet in its gift
and waiting for its chance to breathe.

*

To the grave first
with its square of bluebells
braving their second season,
transplanted from the fields
she walked with Alicia and the dogs,
mixed with others dug
from Múinteoir Mary's front lawn
and more picked this morning
straight from the woods
she scouted with Jack and Niamh.

Next, to the garden created last year
from a corner of scraggly grass
behind the end classroom,

coming back to life now
around the stone table
positioned to catch the sun
with her name on its circular rim,
her final school report
a croí geal fialmhar éadrom óg
curving out of view.

Last, to the seat where she fell,
baby-wiping the white letters
of her plaque at our feet
In honor of ... A loved friend,
then sitting in the blowy sunshine
of this late Spring weekday morning
to look out over the whole pitch
as though at space never before seen
this big and green and empty.

*

The life we have lost
has left a shape
that is curving us
round the bend:

we are hollowed out
to ourselves
by your passing,
though the sea
still knows us
on the shore.

I was standing at the wave line watching the rip of it
—the tide's blue-green surge come shining and chopping
up the crushed dull yellow coral between two arms of rock—
when a gull flew across my line of vision
and I followed it as it turned against the light
and seemed to fade into the sky
even while the shining spot in which I last saw it
was still seagull-separate.

Returning to the car, I stopped to read a monument inscription,
"In memory of all those nameless children
and our people here about
who were swept from us in the time of the great famine
and who are now in the arms of God."

*

This stone
is becoming pliable,
like warmed putty
pinched soft,
its outer layers giving
the fingers plenty to do,
but leadened,
fit for the pockets
of one looking at a river

or like the stone I need,
blunt yet heavy,
to place at the bottom
of a vase of white
double-headed narcissi,
drunken-scented
from the garden,
to stop the wind
blowing it over.

                *

She played it for us so many times—
You'll take the high road and I'll take the low road,
before proudly proclaiming, "I'm one-sixteenth Scots!"
then effortlessly sweep through the tune again.
We always said one day we'd take her there,
even though she told us she'd be there before us.

Now two years on, it's just her father and me
at last arrived on the bonny banks
and dying to meet her again. Listen—unknownst to me
he has carried from home her recorder:
before turning back, we'll send her notes high and clear
till they dissolve over the sleeping water.

*

Beneath Sagrada Familia's
spindling pins,
God the bubble-maker bends
with two sticks and a string
to pull new worlds from a bucket
to hold his breath within
the man, woman and child
here shining in their day—

triptych-trusting they survive
what His love may entail:
beauty's blistering light
against the passion façade
where they're bursting for life
beyond belief, beyond obtain.

*

"You have great faith."

No. I'm paddling a shallow stream
all hung with pussy willows
flowing through fields of willed dreams
on an island adrift in an endless ocean.

I am in fear and trembling, for
it is great to give up one's desire,
but greater still to stick to it
after having given it up, entire.

We have walked into gathering gloom along the tow path,
the light of day on our side diminishing on the water
although it shines again at the far end.

How long this tunnel is! Its perfect curve
drips into the canal, disturbing its own dark mirrored order,
stalactites pointing at softness underfoot.

Deep inside its chamber we begin to sing in a round,
By-i-i-i the wa-a-ters, the wa-a-ters of Babylon,
our voices rebounding, multiplied and returning

to weep for one whose faith we follow in the dark
till the other side is reached.

*

This is a ship of state,
stopped in the mid-Atlantic
on a cold clear night,
listing, holed, broken,
due to slip beneath.

And this is a báidín bídeach,
risen sun gleaming
in the drops
that are beading
every line.

*

We are arriving back at the coast where we were very happy.
I am finding it hard to breathe.

The village sign tells us, "Remember the health of our children."
Small birds chirp in the eaves

above pots of summer planting. We re-enter the only hotel,
its old safe-carpet, small-lobby smell.

I greet the me who used feel for her without thinking on my skin.
"Cloudy, but clearing," the owner says. She doesn't know us.

I close my eyes at the turn of the stairs: my daughter's bare
            legs descend
and I hear a child's sandals slap on the hard surface outside.

We have a room with a view. Its extractor fan hums relentlessly
as he hands me a cup of tea and a custard cream.

The left hand window looks towards the graveyard on the hill,
the right one, to the open sea in its V-shaped cradle.

Later we will swim in it, whole-body lifted on the incoming tide,
our being blessedly no longer our business.

In the morning when we wake, all the shadows of the graves
will point in the other direction,

but for now we must stand by our small tower of stones on
            the beach:
we know one wave with no warning will take it.

In the half-dark of a midsummer's late evening,
the sky over the village unraveling its color bands,
I stand alone at her seat in the playing field
with a watering can and baby wipes in my hands.
I start to spin, gathering speed on the spot where
she was shocked at her last breath here,
my arms outstretched, my body shot through
with new power flowing out of me.
When I suddenly stop, the world stays spinning,
field and village leaping drunkenly
from end to end, sloshing and reeling
in sympathy with me stumbling to see
how I should ever again be stable enough
to hold God's line between the black and the blue.

*

High in the foothills of the Paps,
a goddess waits in her circle of stone
for millennia of pilgrims to pass
through her fires to the city of Shrone.

Tracing her cross in a ring that is worn
deep into rock on her mound of screed,
my hand slips forward as if foreknown
by all like me who've sought her in need.

*

I'd always planned one day to tell her
that her life here on earth began
a week or so before nine-eleven,
still in the age of innocence.
That she was conceived the week before
the war-on-terror's oxymoron
had always seemed to me appropriate
to a child of friendship and play

already using her providential legacy
from a world before global fear
to challenge dread's might and legitimacy—
not knowing she'd ask the same of me.

*

When you speak to her,
let her answer you.

*

Today I sat by your grave and prayed for help:
no matter how this desert has bloomed since you died,
nor how worthy even the cause of your memory,
your absence remains unforgiveable.

Then tonight your father asked me out
to see the low full moon emerge
from between its swags of cloud,
and our friends out late checking sheep, hearing us,
called us up the field to shine a bright torch
high into the ash tree on our boundary ditch,
and showed us a barn-owl and two chicks nesting,
accounting at last for the strange calls
we've heard each dusk up the hill for weeks.

My sweet daughter, you have answered me
in every way you could:
tomorrow we will rediscover your first-class school workbook
where to the set question, "What is your favorite animal?"
you wrote, "A barn owl, though I've never seen one."

*

You recalibrate us anew
to the scale of the robin
          who for one moment—then two
perched alongside us
          on the tail-board of the trailer
in which the gentle body
          of the black ewe you loved,
and who as an orphan lamb
          you named for your kin,
last week was carried home.

*

Gone through into that so complete
she is fully absorbed to it,
what can there be now between my child
and every other living thing?

She is not in my dreams, instead
my dreams are bathed in her
as particles lightly bounce, extending
all that are here or once were.

No boundaries, then, nor blockage
between my child and me?
Yet dreaming so, I am hostage
to death's advanced decree.

*

Weighed down, I put my foot out
over and over to feel this new ground:
moon dust rising on mountains of dreams
and next to no atmosphere.

Peering through perspex at the curve of earth
I thought I'd see at last in the round,
I know the world I've left
still pulls me with it after the sun,

though beyond its sway is a memory
of such deep and unimaginable space,
my consciousness is pushing through
where nothing else can follow.

I look behind me in the car
to the place where she sat,
before me to the sweep of stars.

*

Driving home in the dark
towards a crescent moon
lying in my windscreen
like a young girl in long grass:

dog daisies are nodding
where her hand shades her eyes
against the unseen brilliance
of the daystar light.

*

Waking early, to see the reflection
of a window criss-crossed on the wall
in the shadow dark, and resting,

only later to realize
that this was the light source itself—
the new morning glowing
through an outside door
gone unnoticed the night before.

*

Her essence can no more be
extinguished by her dying
than created by her birth…

*

You do not speak as the shadow bars
of your life in the tomb of life
are broken, as the glow of the risen sun
turns this grey sky blue. Your hidden life
is coming through as a flame
found by the morning star still burning,
now a new heart is put in you.

*

Our daughter was guided by an unseen hand
pulling back on the string of a yawning bow

big as the world she played in, the sun that warmed her,
arms that held her, heart that gave

when the hand let go and her filament of flight
raised our sights to the illimitable.

*

You're a paraglider who'll never now come down,
so many thermals have formed against your life's sheer face
on which the sun has shone all these years,
its decade of stored heat waiting to lift you like a bird.

Traveling with us to the high level slopes of that playing field,
you carried your folded wing so well packed on your back
that we never knew it till you ran across the grass
into pure air. Take-off was easy—you were on earth

and then you weren't, feeling nothing between the two.

I imagine now the snow and rock and scree and glaciers
of our lives below, still insurmountable to us,
dreaming that one day you'll glide low enough to speak to us
still hiking this sharp ridge, at last unburdening as you pass over.

*

We're still here.
          Me too!
How's that, then?
          Not tellin'!

*

Her uncle plants an oak tree
in our garden for her,

"to last five hundred years," he says,
that her memory may renew.
As the seasons pass over it
we will watch its limbs release
more keys to where she is now
than any of us could need.

*

I step out of the car from Dublin
and make my way up the field
in the last light of the summer solstice,
keeping a wary eye on the black sheep
lying in against the ditch for the night
(unused now to our arrivals
and among which is a young ram).
At the highest point I crouch to the grass.

Once before, he and I raced from the city
to make it to this spot at this hour,
stood together in our first year of marriage
and gloried in the gold expanse
of the whole world at our feet,
our only daughter still to be conceived
along with the eleven years thereafter
we would be given to keep her.

He cannot be with me tonight
but I have come to mark this for us both,
even though there is no slow drop
of a pure and unimpeded ball of light
behind the Devil's Bit, extending our day
beyond anything that could have seemed possible.

This time the whole evening sky
must be its own imaginary rainbow, arcing
colorless and wide and mottled
as the breeze scoring a dog's faraway bark
and our neighbor's near-grown lambs, calling.

Hunkered low, my face is touched
by full seed heads; I see more flowers
than we ever imagined surviving here
with the trees on our boundary ditch,
so greenly made-up with themselves
that it's hard to believe that from tonight
they start to throw it all away again.

Our cat comes calling pitifully
to me for his dinner. *All my care.*
I make one wish to go well till winter
and stand up, aching, to lead him home,
passing by the baby horse-chestnut tree
we bought for a fiver one summer fête
and proudly planted by her in our garden,
nearly as tall now as she would be
within its own tightly lawnmowered circle
of sleeping dog daisies and buttercups and clover.

*

It takes five hundred changes to make a *peal*
with no repetition of pattern allowed,
each bell dodging the other's clamorous heels
to swing full circle, yet always return.

So may we learn to live without her here,
ringing the changes the days must bring
to life's score and pattern, her bright spirit leading
new ways to sound out everything.

*

Today I think her face is in the trees,
in the scattered scratching leaves on the ground
in the windy dawn into which I step.
This day is born in the full pink she spurned,
taking whole sections of the dark with it
as dead leaves whirl
below their branches lit in black
and backed by the breaking morning.

*

She has sped so far ahead by now
around the far bends
of the circular walk in the woods
that she's already doing laps:
no sooner passing us
than she comes up behind us
to breathe on the back of our ears,
then dodge sideways, laughing,
before once more showing us
a clean pair of heels…

*

Bending to the sandpit
where our baby girl once played
in the compact city state
of her grandmother's people

warm beneath her bottom,
soft between her toes,
sifting through her fingers
here in kindness truly shown

that we may find her in these grains
cleaving chill to our touch,
who yet must come around
to her still living, having lived

warm beneath our bottom,
soft between our toes,
sifting through our fingers
now in every kindness shown…

*

You're re-absorbed to that place beyond me
that you and I always have known,

where deep in my body's first memory,
my flesh still gives you its word

to love and protect you for ever
though you've scrolled from me free as a bird.

Are you the book of my life then or chapter?
Neither—you're what brings it to bind:

you are the interleaved meaning still hidden
in the spaces between every line.

*

Folding our fairy lights into storage,
she'd first untangle them for me
by backing them through the doorway
on her arms held out as a tree.

I'd then gather each fragile seed
to its bouquet of counterparts
by pulling her back towards me
on a line of unbroken stars.

*

Holy is the bed they rolled your body on
from the Emergency Room to the one they set aside
for our last night together as one family
of father, mother and (just-deceased) child.

Holy the nurse who, when she banged your bed
against the door-jamb leading us in,
in deep reflex instinct for your sacred life
said immediately, "I'm sorry, Emily."

Holy the steps I took from my bed to yours
in the small hours to cradle your strange weight
and holy those that followed to your father's side
who warmed me through while I held your shoulder blade.

Holy the arrival of my sister and my brother
early next day to help us to the city mortuary;
holy the mysteries of the nurses' skill
who made you flexible again for that last journey.

Holy your uncle's upper body strength
who carried you tenderly to the hired car
and placed you in our arms across the back seat,
face to my chest and your hips to your father's.

Holy the sunshine on that early Sunday morning
on the old man sitting outside his front door,
and every quiet word exchanged between us two
as the driver sped along those empty roads.

Holy then, the texture of each of your bare feet
in our last moments with you after arriving,
as one by one, I slipped from them the white socks you'd put on
and covered you with the blanket they'd provided.

Holy at the last the arms that held me up
outside the door I had to leave you behind,
as holy, holy, holy now and always are you—
our beloved, our darling only child.

Our neighbors' hands
weren't sore from writing
(they'd call a spade
neither a spade nor a pen),

but from the shovels and picks
that twelve of them brought
to our new plot,
where they conferred and then,

taking turns to slice roots
and lift clay,
they shaped due form
for my daughter's remains,

going down
for the deep drop needed,
giving me solace
no words can explain.

*

Black, sweet night
thick with mist—
I lift my face to you
mouth-watering
before I go in.

Her Dawn

The child stirs in her early hunger.
I draw east curtains on a thick mist
rolled up to the yard gate and stopped there.
The unseeable field is framed by two trees,
pillars to the throne-room in the boundary ditch
through which her day is coming with magic.
Not a stir from the three sleeping dogs
housed beneath a smoke-orange violet sky.
Not morning, not what I've ever known as dawn,
this world spread before us on our bed throne
in white-dyed wind where not a leaf stirs,
just now dissolving to spread with intent
through the gate barrier towards the silent house
where I hold her who feeds from me still —

(Autumn 2002)

Notes

Part Two of this volume, "Threnodies for Emily," is a sequence of poems written for my daughter, Emily Elise Wilson, who died suddenly of cardiac arrest in May 2013, aged nearly eleven.

"Slievenamon": Slievenamon is a mountain in South Co. Tipperary, a solitary peak overlooking a broad plain. It is associated with the Fenian cycle of mythological tales, and its name translates as "mountain of the women."

"Martha Blake Reprieved": This poem is a response to Austin Clarke's 1963-collected masterpiece, "Martha Blake at Fifty-One," Austin Clarke, *Collected Poems* (Carcanet 2008), 269–274.

"Carved Head at Jerpoint": Jerpoint is a ruined twelfth-century Cistercian abbey near Thomastown, Co. Kilkenny, famous for its stone carvings.

"Kilcooley": Kilcooley is a later twelfth-century daughter foundation of the Cistercian Abbey at Jerpoint, also in ruins. It is situated in southeast Co. Tipperary.

"Passing On the Faith": after Vatican II, the nomenclature "Holy Ghost" was replaced by "Holy Spirit" in common Catholic prayers such as "Glory Be To the Father…". In Ireland, as elsewhere, there was often delay before the liturgical changes associated with Vatican II began to be implemented in ordinary practice.

"Evictions": Barnadown (Barr na dTamhan) is the name of a hilly townland in south Co. Kilkenny that once was part of the estate of Castlemorris, and which was the scene of an infamous mass eviction in the post-famine period. The details of the eviction curse as related in this poem, remain current in local folklore.

The stones of the big house were used after its destruction by former tenants for building and repair purposes.

"Spring Equinox": "fort/da" is Sigmund Freud's name for a game played by his 18-month-old grandson involving a cotton reel which the boy would repeatedly throw out of his cot. "Fort" means "gone" and "da" means "there." The significance of the game, which Freud discusses in "Beyond the Pleasure Principle" (1920), is that it shows the child transforming an unhappy situation, one in which they have no control over the presence of their parents, into a happy one in which the parents are at the beck and call of the child. Freud also interpreted it as a kind of revenge on the parents, a way of saying to them that they aren't so important (source: Oxford Reference.com). Non-transitive dice are irregularly-numbered dice which show that, on average, if die A beats die B and die B beats die C, then A does not beat C as one would expect—rather, C beats A.

"The Stolen Boat": "báidín-ó" translates from the Irish as "little boat."

"At the Site of Bowen's Court": Bowen's Court was the Co. Cork ancestral home of the writer Elizabeth Bowen (1899–1973).

"In this, the longest night of the year in which she died…": Preceded by a number of cool and wet years, the summer of 2013 in Ireland turned out fine and warm. The following winter, the solstice at Newgrange on December 21, 2013 was reported as being "one of the finest—no, the most spectacular—sunrise in living memory" (Eileen Battersby, *The Irish Times*). Soon that same December morning, the weather turned stormy again.

"Poll na Brón—its capstone's massive slant": The Poulnabrone (Poll na Brón) Dolmen is found in the Burren, Co. Clare. "Poll na Brón" translates directly as "the hole of sorrow."

"To the grave first…": "Múinteoir" is the Irish word for teacher; "a croí geal fialmhar éadrom óg" translates approximately as follows: "her young heart, so bright and generous and free."

"I was standing at the wave line watching the rip of it…": the beach in this poem is Féile an Dóilín (the Coral Strand) near An Ceathrú Rua, Co. Galway. The monument there marks a grave (killeen) for unbaptized children. Its inscription in the original Irish reads: "Trá na bPáistí / Cumhdaite / I mbaclainn Muire / Go luídh, a Thiarna, / Ár naíonáin gan ainm / Is ár ngaolta caoine / Sciobad uainn / Le linn an Ghorta Mhóir / Pobal an ceantair a tós an leacht seo / 1997." Its partial translation in this poem is by the present author.

"This is a ship of state…": the phrase "báidín bídeach" translates as "tiny boat." This is the opening phrase in the chorus of the well-known Irish-language song, "Báidín Fheilimí."

Acknowledgments

Some of these poems, in either the present or earlier versions, have appeared in the following publications: *Boyne Berries*; *Crannóg*; *Cyphers*; *Ghosts in my Heels* (chapbook by Catriona Clutterbuck, 2005); *Oxford Poetry*; *Oxford Poets 2007: An Anthology* (eds. David Constantine and Bernard O'Donoghue, 2007); Oxfam Ireland *Poems for 2006* (Calendar); *Poetry Ireland Review*; *Staying Human* (ed. Neil Astley, 2020); *The Blue Nib*; *The Honest Ulsterman*; *The Kilkenny Anthology* (ed. MacDara Woods, 1991); *The May Anthology of Oxford and Cambridge Poetry* (ed. Seamus Heaney, 1993); *The Steeple*; *Windows Authors and Artist Introductions Series* (ed. Heather Brett, 1994); AnamCara Website (Irish Parental Bereavement Association); AnamCara Information Leaflet, "Living With No Surviving Children" (2017).

I thank all those who have read and responded to many of these poems over the years, especially Deirdre Brennan, Denis Collins (RIP), Carmel Cummins, Kerry Hardie, Pat Maddock, Pat Murphy, Olivia O'Leary, Mark Roper, Larry Stapleton (RIP), and Jean Valentine. In particular, I owe a major debt of gratitude to those who have read drafts of the sequence "Threnodies for Emily," and whose commentary, advice, and encouragement in relation to it have been invaluable. In this regard, I am especially grateful to Jefferson Holdridge, Lucy Collins, Paula Meehan, and Bernard O'Donoghue, who between them have responded to the sequence across a number of its incarnations. Above all, I thank Emily's father, my husband Nic, whose presence by me has been central to the writing of these poems, as to so much else.